The Elements in Poetry

AIR

Published in 2007 by Evans Brothers Limited
2A Portman Mansions
Chiltern St
London W1U 6NR

British Library Cataloguing in Publication Data
Air. - (The elements of poetry)
    1. Air - Juvenile poetry
    I. Peters, Andrew (Andrew Fusek)
    808.8'1936

    ISBN-10: 0237528886
13-digit ISBN 9780237528881

Editorial: Julia Bird & Su Swallow
Design: Simon Borrough
Production: Jenny Mulvanny

Contents

Breathing Cinquains

Draw air
Through nose or mouth
To trachea, bronchi,
Bronchioles, to alveoli.
Let breath

Release
Into your blood
Oxygen, and take back
Waste gas your body does not need.
Breathe out.

Empty
Alveoli
Through bronchioles, bronchi,
Trachea. Use air power to speak,
Sing, shout.

Alison Chisholm

The Adventures of Oxygen

O
to
be
like
OX
Y   Y
G   G
N   E   E   N

that rushes to a lung to catch the pul-monary vein for travelling is fun! Especially when you're soaked in blood and off to find a heart – exploring auri-cles and valves and ventricles is part of being the sort of oxy-gen that sails the great aorta rides arteries, capil-laries

to cells and cer-tain slaugh-ter for cells will gobble oxygen then belch out nasty gas that travels on the next vein back back to the pear shaped mass of muscle pumping dirty blood into the start-ing lung, where nasty gasses must get off – make way for

♥
x
y
g
e
n

Gina Douthwaite

Facts About Air

Scientists say
That air consists
Of about 78% nitrogen and 21% oxygen
Plus some carbon dioxide
And small amounts
Of the rare gases - helium, argon and neon.

These are facts, I know.
But I also know
That when I go outside
On a spring morning
The air tastes as crisp
As a fresh lettuce
And that when I sit
On the patio
On a summer evening
The cool night air
Brushes my cheek like a feather.

John Foster

LISTEN

Shhhhhhhhhhhhhhhhhhh!
Sit still, very still
And listen.
Listen to wings
Lighter than eyelashes
Stroking the air.
Know what the thin breeze
Whispers on high
To the coconut trees.
Listen and hear.

Telcine Turner

THE BALLOON MAN

The balloon man stands
In the town square.
Winter and summer
He's always there

With a bunch of balloons
All sizes and shapes:
Sausages and hearts,
Rhinos and apes;

And every colour
You've ever seen:
Silver and violet,
Orange and green.

He holds them
Like a big bouquet
As they tug and bounce
And bump and sway.

One windy morning
He wasn't there:
His balloons had lifted him
High in the air

And carried along
By the wind's force,
He waved down to the crowd –
One-handed, of course.

Then he took from his pocket
A pin made of gold,
Began bursting balloons –
Just a few – and behold:

Down he came gently,
Just floating on air,
To the cheering of children
In the town square.

Eric Finney

S
E
S
I
R
R
I
A
T
cOld air doesn't
H

Lisa Watkinson

What Wood Wind Do?

Here's the trick,
Breathe in quick,
Then you take
The silver snake
Raise to lip
Let breath rip
Air vibrates
resonates
I salute
The singing flute!

Rosalind Peters (aged 10)

Bluebottle

Who dips, dives,
swoops out of space,
a buzz in his wings
and sky on his face;
now caught in the light,
now gone without trace,
a sliver of glass,
never still in one place?

Who's elusive as a pickpocket,
lord of the flies;
who moves like a rocket,
bound for the skies?
Who's catapult, aeroplane,
always full-throttle?
Sky-diver, Jumping Jack,
comet,
bluebottle!

Judith Nicholls

Wind Forces - The Beaufort Scale

In force one, weather vanes won't stir
But chimney smoke will drift.
In force two, vanes will gently turn,
Leaves rustle, petals lift.

In force three, leaves and small twigs bend,
A long and thin branch sways.
Force four; flags ruffle in the breeze,
Pollen and dust are raised.

In force five, small trees whip and toss
And clouds sail through the sky.
Force six; umbrellas blow away,
Winds whistle, skirt hems fly.

In seven, whole trees bend and lurch
And washing lines come down.
Force eight; it's really hard to walk,
Branches can smash the ground.

Force nine will lift the tiles off roofs
And chimney pots will fall.
Force ten uproots a chestnut tree,
Rips fences, knocks down walls.

Eleven is a violent storm,
Destroys a crop of grain.
Force twelve can lay the land to waste -
We call it hurricane.

Celia Gentles

Hurricane

Next time a hurricane comes
   banging at my door
ripping up my tin roof
raining on my floor,
   next time a hurricane comes
   tearing up my trees
breaking down my fences
or stirring up the seas,
  be they Frances, Jeanne or Barry
Humberto or Edouard,*
I'll stick my finger in their eye
and poke 'em real hard.

Doda Smith

*Storms are named alphabetically as they happen.
The same names are reused every six years.

TORNADO

I'm a joyrider. I'm a twister.
Give up now. You can't resist.
Gun-slinger. Car-slinger too.
Watch out! I'll wake you and take you
and shake you about. Like a massive bonfire
in the distance. I take the line
of no resistance. Sharpshooter,
house looter, on the run.
Get in my way
and it won't be fun.
In my eye
it's as quiet
as a mouse.
Next minute
I'll destroy
your house.
Hide in the
cellar. Hide
in the bath.
I'll find you
if you're in
my path.
I'm a
tornado
bent on
trouble.
Behind me
is only
a pile
of
rubble.

Jill Townsend

The Old Windmill

Catch the wind, just for an instant
Catch the wind, then let it go
Take a breath from nature's forces
Snatch it from the winds that blow

Catch the wind, with wood and canvas
Massive sails stretch and fill
Slow and creaking, faster, stronger
Breathing life into the mill

Ancient beams transmit the motion
Wood-hewn bearings slap and moan
Pulleys lift, and gear-wheels trundle
Powering the wheel of stone

Grain is caught, and crushed, and powdered
Sacks are filled, and stored for need
Winds that once caressed the wheat field
Grind the goodness from the seed

Catch the wind, just for a moment
Catch the wind, then let it go
Yesterday, today, tomorrow
Power from the winds that blow

Paul Bright

THE MERRY-GO-ROUND SONG

What shall we do with the ozone layer?
What shall we do, Daddy dear?
We'll knit the clouds into tight white shrouds
And stitch it with needles of fear.

The clock is striking, oh is it too late?
Have we run out of time, Mummy dear?
With our ladder of cars, we shall climb to the stars
To create a new atmosphere.

But when will we learn the lesson we must?
When will we learn, brother dear?
We will learn how to fly like a plane in the sky
What a gas! {that won't disappear.}

And is the earth leaking and what of her wounds?
Oh what of her wounds, sister dear?
To plug up the hole, we shall fill it with coal
Though it bleeds with a dark oily smear.

What shall we do with the ozone layer?
Don't worry your head, my dear
Now hide your tears and close up your ears
For nobody wants to hear.

Andrew Fusek Peters

Bully

The wind is making everything unhappy,
Big noise, throwing its weight about.

We know it by twigs in a twist,
Butterflies driven backwards;

By geraniums in tatters,
Windows' rattling panic;

By whipping washing, old men
Duffed up against the wall.

It taunts and chivvies us,
Drum and bass too loud for comfort.

Give it something to play with ~ a turbine
Spinning energy to keep us warm.

Carole Satyamurti

WIND FARM HAIKUS

A silver forest
Of trunks spears sky. Angled boughs
Sweep stiff, catch the wind.

No sap ooze, no
Leaves curl; but the forest yields
Electric harvest.

Alison Chisholm

WHAT ARE THUNDER AND LIGHTNING MADE OF?

Storm cloud, storm cloud, angry and mean
Storm cloud, storm cloud, where have you been?
I have ridden and battled up here in the sky
Long have I fought and loud was my cry.

Storm cloud, storm cloud, cruel dark shade,
Storm cloud, tell me, how were you made?
Fire and ice were part of the potion:
Warm air plus cold cloud equals commotion.
Heated air rises, expanded and free;
Bumps into icy cold: that's what makes me!

Storm cloud, storm cloud, awesome it's true,
Storm cloud, storm cloud, then what do you do?
Ice crystals smash against warmth in attack,
A battle so fierce, it ends with a crack;
As electrical charges build to a crash
And static rips out as a lightning flash.

Storm cloud, storm cloud, nature's freak,
Storm cloud tell me, how do you speak?
Air, *heated by lightning bursts outward as thunder*
I *sing of the surge of electrical wonder.*

Polly Peters

Look at the cloud-cat lapping there on high
With lightning tongue the moon-milk
From the sky!

Kalidasa

Kite Flight

A windy day on Crocker's Hill
Cloud chases cloud across the sky;
Today my kite should heed my will;
Today's the day for it to fly.

And so it does: it soars up high,
Then briefly dips to rise again,
And I can see its pigtails fly
And feel the tight string's eager strain.

It pulls and jerks as if I held
An eager greyhound on a lead;
A mighty tug and I'm compelled
Almost to see the wild thing freed.

Not quite! I grip with all my might
And think for one mad moment I
Could be dragged upward by my kite
To dangle in astonished sky.

But no, there is a sudden lull;
The wind decides to stand at ease,
And like a swooping hawk or gull
My kite speeds down towards the trees.

Luckily it skims their tops
And arrows back to Crocker's Hill;
It hits the ground, then twitches, flops,
A stranded fish, and then lies still.

Vernon Scannell

MIGRATION

Swallows gorge on mosquito and midge.
Autumn is on the wing
Drawing near. Memories of the south nudge
Instinct, a gravitational pull
Of sunfilled African song.
Over an unknown distance, they hear its call.

Answer with hieroglyphics on telegraph wires. Soon.
We'll come, they say, when trees say it's time.
When leaf dances with leaf we'll look for the sign
Of sea being greyer, a blue day that's shorter,
Then shake the north from our feathers. Head home.
Follow the slip-stream of summer over the water.

Catherine Benson

The Windhover

I caught this morning morning's minion, king-
dom of daylight's dauphin, dapple-dawn-drawn Falcon, in his riding
Of the rolling level underneath him steady air, and striding
High there, how he rung upon the rein of a wimpling wing
In his ecstasy! Then off, off forth on swing,
As a skate's heel sweeps smooth on a bow-bend: the hurl and gliding
Rebuffed the big wind. My heart in hiding
Stirred for a bird, - the achieve of, the mastery of the thing.

Brute beauty and valour and act, oh, air, pride, plume, here
Buckle! AND the fire that breaks from thee then, a billion
Times told lovelier, more dangerous, O my chevalier!

No wonder of it: shéer plód makes plough down sillion
Shine, and blue-bleak embers, ah my dear,
Fall, gall themselves, and gash gold-vermillion.

Gerard Manley Hopkins

GLIDERS

Hoist them up, let go
The rope, just so
They hang there
Balancing on air.

The Sunday sky
Is suddenly
Full of them, their slim
Bodies, delicate and trim.

Such an intense,
Mysterious silence,
Such a slow, weightless,
Gradual progress.

Almost they repose
Above their own shadows,
Almost they keep
Watch over their own sleep,

Until with a sudden
Wakeful dipping down
They seem
As if snatched from a dream

To obey once more
The weekday law
Of nose to the ground,
Deadweight, earthbound.

John Mole

The Montgolfiers' Recipe 1783

Take one basket.
Attach a paper balloon.
Heat slowly over a charcoal fire
Till hot air rises.
Add one basket one cockerel,
One sheep and a duck.
Release in front of a crowd
And King Louis XVI of France.
Float for 8 minutes.
Allow to land gently.
Release creatures,
Unharmed.

Clap.
Sing.
Dance.

Celia Warren

To the Thawing Wind

COME with rain. O loud Southwester!
Bring the singer, bring the nester;
Give the buried flower a dream;
Make the settled snowbank steam;
Find the brown beneath the white;
But whate'er you do tonight,
Bathe my window, make it flow,
Melt it as the ice will go;
Melt the glass and leave the sticks
Like a hermit's crucifix;
Burst into my narrow stall;
Swing the picture on the wall;
Run the rattling pages o'er;
Scatter poems on the floor;
Turn the poet out of door.

Robert Frost

If, all of a sudden, air wasn't there

If, all of a sudden, air wasn't there
Our cheeks would turn blue as a squad car's light;
We'd gasp like Grandpa on the topmost stair

After the climb to his bedroom at night.
And what of the plight of creatures that fly?
They would be stuck without rockets for flight!

And under the freezing and pitch black sky
Earth plants would wither and never revive.
There'd be no fireworks or burning the Guy -

No bonfire flame or flare could contrive
To combust – like us they too need to breathe.
(Only aliens who'd learnt to survive

In vacuums would be there to lay Earth's wreath!)

Philip Waddell

Author Index

Acknowledgements

Catherine Benson: 'Migration', by permission of the author.
Alison Chisholm: 'Breathing Cinquains' and 'Wind Farm Haikus', by permission of the author.
Gina Douthwaite: 'The Adventures of Oxygen' by Gina Douthwaite. First published in *Picture a Poem*, Hutchinson Children's Books, 1994.
Eric Finney: 'The Balloon Man', © Eric Finney. By permission of the author.
John Foster: 'Facts About Air', © John Foster, from *Standing on the Sidelines* (Oxford University Press), included by permission of the author.
Robert Frost: 'To the Thawing Wind', from *The Poetry of Robert Frost*, edited by Edward Connery Lathem, published by Jonathan Cape. Reprinted by permission of The Random House Group Ltd.
Celia Gentles: 'Wind Forces – The Beaufort Scale', by permission of the author.
John Mole: 'Gliders', from *The Dummy's Dilemma* (Hodder, 1999), by permission of the author.
Judith Nicholls: 'Bluebottle', © 1994 Judith Nicholls, from *Storm's Eye* by Judith Nicholls, published by Oxford University Press. Reprinted by permission of the author.
Andrew Fusek Peters: 'The Merry-Go-Round Song', © Andrew Fusek Peters. By permission of the author.
Polly Peters: 'What are Thunder and Lightning Made Of?' © Polly Peters. By permission of the author.
Rosalind Peters: 'What Wood Wind Do?' © Rosalind Peters. By permission of the author.
Carole Satyamurti: 'Bully', first appeared in *Poetry Review*. By permission of the author.
Vernon Scannell: 'Kite Flight', by permission of the author.
Doda Smith: 'Hurricane', © Doda Smith. By permission of the author.
Jill Townsend: 'Tornado', © Jill Townsend 2006. By permission of the author.
Lisa Watkinson: 'Air', by permission of the author.
Philip Waddell: 'If, All of a Sudden, Air Wasn't There', by permission of the author
Celia Warren: 'The Montgolfiers' Recipe 1783', by permission of the author.

Every effort has been made to trace the copyright holders, but in some cases this has not proved possible. The publisher will be happy to rectify any such errors or omissions in future reprints and/or new editions.

Picture credits

Cover: © royalty-free Corbis; p.6: © Irina Tischenko/istockphoto; p.8 © Danish Khan/istockphoto; p.9: © Nina Lao/istockphoto; p.10-11: © Alan Schein Photography/Corbis; p.13: © Laurie Knight/istockphoto; p.14-15: © Corbis; p.17: © Ludovic Maisant/Corbis; p.19: © Gunter Marx Photography/Corbis; p.20: © Steve Rabin/istockphoto; p.22: Peggy Heard; Frank Lane Photography Agency/Corbis; p.23: © photolibrary.com; p.25: © Leonard de Selva/Corbis; p.26: © Matthew Scherf/istockphoto; p.27: istockphoto

THE ELEMENTS IN POETRY

Poems from the other books in this series

THE FLIGHT OF ICARUS

I rose on wings of wax,
Tracing angel tracks.

The sun called out my name
And I took reckless aim

Upward - the chosen one
First to kiss the Sun!

I started to perspire
In universal fire,

As if God struck a match
And somehow I could catch

Its light and hold it long…
I was wrong.

J PATRICK LEWIS

Taken from **Fire** ISBN 0 237 52885 1 (13-digit ISBN 978 0 237 52885 0)

Rain in the City

I had only known the splash
and the pelt and the scatter,
the gush and the gurgle of gutters
and the tumbled drums of the thunder –
until I looked downwards from an upstairs
office-block
and saw the sudden flowering
a thousand umbrellas
in a most unlikely spring.

Anne Bell

Taken from **Water** ISBN ISBN 0 237 52886 X (13-digit 978 0 237 52886 7)

THE GOOD EARTH

More precious than gold,
Some call it mud
But earth makes bodies
Bone and blood.
It grows the plants
Which feed us all
So, birds and beasts,
Both large and small
Come from earth
As humans do.
Earth has grown
Me and you.
More precious than gold,
Don't call it mud,
Call it bodies,
Bone and blood.

Marian Swinger

Taken from **Earth** ISBN 0 237 52887 8 (13-digit ISBN 978 0 237 52887 4)

About the anthologist

Andrew Fusek Peters, together with his wife Polly, has written and edited over 45 books for young people. Their last two verse collections were nominated for the Carnegie Medal and his poems have been recorded for the Poetry Archive (www.poetryarchive.org). His collection Mad, Bad & Dangerously Haddock features the best of his poetry for children over the last 20 years and his anthology Sheep Don't Go To School has been recommended by QCA as part of their Reading Differences scheme. Out of Order, his last anthology for the Evans Publishing Group, was highly praised.

"…an experienced and accomplished anthologist" TES

"His anthologies are always surprising and interesting. He's done it again…" Books for Keeps five star review.

Andrew is also an experienced schools' performer, quite a good juggler and mean didgeridoo player. Check him out on www.tallpoet.com.